Following My Heart
By Anchilada

*Once again this goes out to EVERYONE who has made it possible by believing in me.
Including my Aunt Steffy; thanks for the prompt that became "Truth Is Perception."
Anchilada*

Embrace

My head on your chest
Eyes closed and time still; for one
Moment you are mine

Broken Record

I keep telling you
But you don't want to hear it
From the likes of me

I Know You

I know you Love.
I just haven't met you in person.

I am your biggest fan (I think)…
I know where and when you have touched other people's lives,
I know how you act in public through your many interviews,
I have memorized my favorite lines form your performances.

I know when you did side projects with different celebrities,
(As a potential career change or for charity) you are SO multitalented
I even know what your closest friends said (or are supposed to have said)
About you

I know about your many admirers and which ones you are really close to
The ones who stayed friends and the ones you are just polite with at dinner
parties.
I've even seen places you have lived, even though that was just on T.V.

I know your hobbies and background and we share similar tastes…
So the only thing I don't know is
Why haven't we ever met?

Sculptor

Accept me for whom
I am and I will be glad
To make adjustments

Calm

After a frustrating day
Of not being able to say
Exactly what I feel in fear
Of losing my only career

I finally get home
Lonely and alone
Bored out of my mind
Until I finally try

Lying down on my bed
Setting down my head
On a pillow, pretending it's you
Wondering what you would say or do

Until I start to drift off to sleep
And, sometimes, begin to weep
Because it's NOT you
And there's nothing I can do

To stop the emotions from there
It's just feels so unfair
I start to think of everything else
I thought I had put up on a shelf

I calm down so much I can no longer fight
And the nightmares haunt me the rest of the night
But when they are over I first feel a bit tired
Then, more often than not, truly inspired

From an article published Feb 14th last year in The Journal of Professional Hopeless Romanticism:

Love Autopsy
Or
"Death by Unrequited Love"
By Angela Nichols, PHR

"And then, there's another kind of love: the cruelest kind. The one that almost kills its victims. It's called unrequited love. Of that I am an expert. Most love stories are about people who fall in love with each other. But what about the rest of us? What about our stories, those of us who fall in love alone? We are the victims of the one sided affair. We are the cursed of the loved ones. We are the unloved ones, the walking wounded."

I was recently in Stage 3 of being a Pro HR (please see Stages of Being a Professional Hopeless Romantic) when, during the coping process, I heard this quote. I was then able to head a study on the subject. Some cases that stood out for me were:

Eponine, shot protecting the man she loves, dies in his arms at scene.
Garth, shot in a thunderstorm by woman tired of his cheating
Carmen, shot so she could not be involved with anyone else

Official findings: No one has died from unrequited love on its own.

Treatment options: Get the feelings out any way you feel comfortable... preferably to the person in question. Be aware, however, that most 'relationship' words; 'boyfriend' 'love' 'marriage' 'commitment' etc, have too much stereotypical baggage to properly express these feelings.

I recommend a method called 'the three Cs'; Connection, Contentment, Conversation.

Connection: Look at how much you have in common. This will show you how you feel about the person they were.
Contentment: Look at how comfortable you feel in their presence. This will tell you how you feel about the person they are.
Conversation: Look at your 'line of communication.' How often do you talk and about what? This will tell you about how things will possibly go in the future.

Role Playing

Breathe in, breathe out: collect each tear
Things might not be the way you think
Like one of those RPG games you had better save everything you find along the way
Never know when you might need it

Maybe those tears will buy you a key that opens a door that lets you find your true love
Maybe they will just be traded for a sword to help you defeat a monster
And Loneliness is one hell of a monster

Why do I keep letting it get to me?
Maybe I need to travel to another village with a special book store and find a volume on the subject
Inside will be a note from the previous reader guiding me to a place I will meet them and add them to my Group

Maybe it doesn't even matter because in the end I will have to take on the villain all alone
So I have to keep going through the same places, battling the same minions, until I even level up enough to take on any stage bosses…

Then there are the puzzles… all of these damn puzzles
Missing a piece of a picture here, missing a point to the game here, don't have a member of my Group who can use that spell on this one
Feels like I'm stuck and don't have a Strategy Guide

Why do I even go on?
Because I know the game is programmed to have a way out, an ending where I WIN
It will be SO satisfying when I get there… in the meantime I just want to pitch this damn controller into the television set

Just A Dream?

If this is just a dream, how is it I can?
Hear you so clearly…
See you in my mind…
Smell you in the bedding…
Taste you…
Feel…

Resolution

New Year, same old thing;
Superficial tolerance
I don't need that shit

I Want To Learn

I want to learn how to not ever think of "him".
He is the one I think of when I hear the song "Bleeding Love."

I want to learn how to not hold on to my crushes.
Holding on to them only keeps crushing me.

I want to learn how to express myself.
I still don't say everything I feel out of a sense of fear.

I want to learn how to dance.
I don't try because I don't think I can do it justice.

I want to learn to just be more assertive.
I am way too passive and don't ever want to be aggressive.

I want to learn more about myself from the outside.
People let me get close enough to know me, but don't let me know them.

Sometimes I want to learn how not to want what the world says I should
want just because it says I should.

Someday I will find the teacher who can teach me all of these things.

In the meantime, I want to learn how not to keep going back to this place in
my mind.

Truth Is Perception

Truth is perception, you say? As in ONLY perception…?
I respectfully disagree.

I can see what you were trying to say. That just because I perceive
something one way doesn't mean that is the way it is.
Is the glass half full or half empty?

There is reality to consider:

Truth: people die.
The Titanic did sink, the World Trade Center did get blown up, Hitler had a
lot of people killed.
My mom, my guiding light, is gone.

Truth: people lie.
Doesn't matter if they are known all over the world or are personally in your
life; lies hurt someone, somewhere.
Especially if you lie to yourself; start doing that and you will be lost.

Hell, if truth is only perception I would have… wait.
I am not about to just toss away the key to my most prized possession.
You want to know my truth; you earn it.

A Fan

I am inspired by you.

Every word out of your mouth is food for thought.

Words that make me think of laughing, words that make me think of other points of view, words that make me think of silent moments.

I hear your truth in everything you do.

I see the way you treat people and know you are as generous as you can be, given that no one can be everywhere.

The more I know the more I want to know, and I can just imagine how well you treat your loved ones…

What I am trying to say is: you are one of my favorite fans… and I guess I am a fan of yours too!

Eponine

She always wondered how he became so destitute he needed to enter her world.

She knew she was destitute; everyone treated her kind like vermin. He was more like someone's discarded pet, but he didn't avoid her.
She opened up to him out of a need for connection and a hope of reciprocation.
In an act of pure masochism she agreed to help him connect with another.

She couldn't bear the thought of him being unhappy.
In fact when he became so unhappy he went to risk his life, she did not leave him to it alone.
She took a bullet meant for him.

I have never been in that place, because her spirit is dead in me.
I refuse to settle for something that will only make me sacrifice my "self."

I have worked too hard to discover it.

Frozen

Here comes another disappointment.

It washes over me like a wave of ice cold water trying to freeze me.
I can't get out of its way; parts of my life are already frozen.

I am frozen in a job that is not creatively satisfying; I need it to pay the bills.

I am frozen in a thirteen year olds mindset; getting excited over every tiny thing and getting distracted from my responsibilities.

At least I know I am not alone in feeling this is bullshit.
At least I know that when I set pen to paper I still release the warmer emotions.

As long as my inner core, my heart, stays warm I have a chance of breaking out of the ice.

Curious

I wonder if a
Real kiss melts as easily
As a chocolate one

Poet

Poet, I want to be your poem.

To have you think of me night or day
Guiding me along my way
Protecting me, perfecting me
Never once neglecting me

I want to see you perform me
I want to see how my words move you; watch the changes in your expressions.

I want to hear you recite me
I want to notice the inflections that reflect your feelings

I want to taste the nourishment giving me attention brings
I want to know how satisfied my development makes you

I want to know I have touched you
That you think enough of me to need to express me

I want to breathe in the audience reaction
Knowing you have shown them a piece of "us"

I am here, if you want to take the time to write me down.

Self-Medication

I don't even want
Your PICTURE to see me with
Yet another sweet…

He-LLO!

Do you like it when
I pay attention to you?
I feel the same way…

Fairy Tale

There are times I feel like I will never have a Fairy Tale:

Like a female Beast, the sister of Quasimodo
Like Cinderella never being visited by her Fairy Godmother
Like Snow White not getting away from the Queen
Like Sleeping Beauty never waking up

Other times I feel as if that is a good thing:

No monsters to slay, no magic spells to break
No midnight deadline to leave me longing
No Prince to depend on for my survival
No one depending on me for their future

Yet:

Beast still knew how to love
Cinderella still found peace
Snow White still had comfort
Sleeping Beauty was still cared for

I need someone to see the person I am inside
To look for me because they want to see if I fit
To satisfy our mutual interest
To awaken my true self

Recovery

There are many kinds of injuries.

Mental, when you wind up asking yourself if you are thinking too much
Physical, when you end up in the hospital
Emotional, when you break down and cry

You can always relax your mental state.
Bodies have a surprising way of mending.

Hearts, on the other hand, don't completely mend, so to speak.
All you can do for them is find the right treatment regimen that helps in the
process. It is the heart that most shapes you; all of the things you have gone
through have made you who you are and determine who you will become
based on how you follow future feelings.

Where Do I Run?

When nothing seems to be going my way
When there's no sunshine to brighten my day
When life is not any fun
Where do I run?

Some people run to people, but what if they push you away?
Some people run to their pets, but pets have nothing to say
Some people run to things and money, but those run out fast
Some people run to food, but again that doesn't last

Some argue 'why run at all? Why not stand and fight'?
I'll bet they've never had to outlast an entire night

So I find myself running to my mind
But even there I often find
The shadows will still chase you
And there's nothing you can do

So I guess the answer is that I try my best
Just to find a place safe enough to rest

Venting

I need the sadness
To leave me so I don't let
It poison my soul

Waves

A beach:

A couple silhouetted against the full moon

The moon and stars gone

Lit up by a gaudy boardwalk

As seen through a cozy cottage window

Through a patch of winter trees

Through the boardwalk, lights out, rides broken

A lone woman, sunbathing

Relationship

When I hear the word relationship many images come to mind.
Images of what Society claims define the word.

Dating
Sex
Marriage (including who you can and can not marry and what benefits you
can only get if you follow the rules)

The images mean nothing to me.
They are like words in a storybook with no pictures to a 2 year old.
I don't really know what they mean, I just know how I feel when someone
reads to me. So I carry it everywhere, even hand it to strangers, hoping they
will read to me.

It's easier for the 2 year old. For a little while yet they won't know what 'my
way' really is, or have to deal with the fact they will barely ever get it.

Intervention

I have 'a friend'

She has several addictions and I want to stage an intervention.

She is addicted to creative stimulation.
She can't get through an hour of work without wishing she wasn't there.
How is she going to financially survive if she loses the job?

She is addicted to attention.
Time after time she chases after it with people who couldn't care any less.
Time after time she comes down off the high and cries her eyes out.

She is addicted to her imagination.
She will talk and talk about situations that never happened to her.
Is she losing her hold on reality?

Sometimes she hides as hard as she can just to sneak another high.

Please help me.

Detective

"What's on your mind, doll?"

She blinked and tilted her head as if coming to a decision.

"I think I will sit down and have some brandy after all... if the offer is still good."

So I poured her a brandy and she took it, in both hands, and sat down on the sofa across the room. I sat at my desk.

She took a sip, but didn't take her eyes off of the fire.

"Its times like this I miss my mother. SHE would have known JUST what to do."

We talked for a couple of hours. She put the empty glass down and leaned back in the cushion. Every time we got together it ended with her bringing up her boyfriend. This time was no different...

"Thank you for the drink and for listening... I have to go. Ken will be waiting for me..."

I thought, who are you trying to remind? Me or yourself? but I didn't say anything.

Susan walked the two blocks from his office. She couldn't quite figure out what it was about him that made him so easy to be comfortable around. Sure, they grew up in the same town but their social circles hadn't intersected until recently. She looked up at her window in the apartment building she and Ken lived in feeling a little let down.

When Susan got to her apartment, she checked her answering machine.

"Hi, Suze... it's Ken. I'd really like to see you tonight, so give me a call if you feel up to going out to dinner, ok?"

"I'm sorry, but I don't tonight" she said aloud to the empty room.

The next night, she showed up in my office again. Only this time, the news caught me off guard.

"Ken and I had a huge fight." She shook her head. "I just couldn't..." She looked at the fire. "...connect with him anymore. It was like what I said, or did, or wanted went in one ear and out the other."

I sat down next to her long enough to make eye contact because she wasn't crying and I wanted to get a read on her.

"Looks like you have the situation under control."

I, on the other hand, wanted a drink.

As I downed the brandy (it was the last of that bottle anyway) I could feel her watching me.

"Hey... what's wrong?"

"I want to kill Ken."

She smiled. Then she laughed.

"Ok, then don't tell me... I appreciate the sentiment, but I'm a big girl."

I watched her leave the office and looked at the file on my desk one last time. I had some packing to do.

The next afternoon Susan decided to stop by his office and see if he wanted to have lunch together. When she got there the door was locked and the lights out; meaning, by the unusual-for-him-not-to-be-there time, that he was out of town on a case.

Suppressing a twinge of the what-about-me's she went across the street and got lunch for herself.

It was what he did, she reminded herself. She wouldn't want someone telling her she could or couldn't do something... and since when did she get so possessive? And of him, of all people?

"You're the idiot who stayed with Ken for so long AFTER it was no longer working" she said under her breath.

I ended up staying out of town another week. Nice to get the extra pay but I just wanted to clean up, relax, and go to bed.

I checked my office answering machine remotely.

One number popped up a few times, no messages. I recognized it, so I called.

"Hi, this is Sue. I'm not by my phone right now. Please leave a message."

"Hi... Just got back in town and was checking my messages."

What the hell...

"How about meeting me for lunch tomorrow?"

Sue knocked on his office door before opening it a crack.

"Hello?"

She saw him at his desk, on the phone, one finger up in the 'give me a minute' gesture. He finished and turned to look at her.

"Hey there."

"I didn't know what you'd want to eat..."

He got up and grabbed his coat and they ended up at the diner across from his office. She had a hard time not asking a zillion questions about his case, and he didn't seem to want to talk about it anyway. What they did talk about had an easy ebb and flow. At the end she felt she hadn't been TOO nosy and took away a warm feeling of calm knowing he was ok.

I sat in my office later that night finishing up everything about my last case. Then I got my coat and headed home, thinking of Sue of all things. It's not that she was never on my radar, but she was always on the edge. Timing never worked right, which actually made it easier to talk to her. On the other hand she did that typical not-saying-everything thing women do. I guess I could see where a woman doesn't want to be hurt any more than a man (damned if I was going to be a rebound guy) but... Come. ON!
I had been burned before too.
It was a good thing the flame on whatever-this-was was set on low. Heard about stuff like this; could be interesting.

Someday…

Just because I want
To share with you doesn't mean
You WON'T share with me…

www.ingramcontent.com/pod-product-compliance
Lightning Source LLC
Chambersburg PA
CBHW030010040426
42337CB00012BA/728